Original title:
Verses from Venus

Copyright © 2025 Creative Arts Management OÜ
All rights reserved.

Author: Matthew Whitaker
ISBN HARDBACK: 978-1-80567-787-1
ISBN PAPERBACK: 978-1-80567-908-0

Rhapsody of the Enchanted Skies

The clouds wear hats of fuzzy fluff,
As breezes giggle, oh so tough.
A moonbeam dances, trips on a star,
And dust from comets is the new bizarre.

With winks from planets, a cosmic tease,
They trade their secrets, float with ease.
A space cat yawns, chases a light,
In zero gravity, all takes flight.

Heartbeats Among the Stars

A nebula's wig, it's colorful flair,
Rocks in space do the tango, fair!
Stars wink coyly, making it snappy,
While aliens giggle, feeling quite happy.

The Milky Way spills soda pop,
With meteors zooming, never a flop.
Hearts beat loudly in rhythm galore,
Unruly cosmos, we all adore.

Sonnet of the Solar Embrace

In sunshine's hug, we jump and twirl,
Planets wave back, giving a whirl.
A comet's tail is a feathered quill,
Writing jokes in space, what a thrill!

The sun tells puns, they dance like rays,
Laughing with laughter that lights our days.
Gravity's a friend, but sometimes it's mean,
When socks float away, it's quite the scene!

Moonlit Dreams and Stardust Wishes

Beneath the moon in a goofy trance,
Stars hold hands, engaging in dance.
A wish on stardust, oh what a game,
But wishes go wild, and all feel the same.

The night sky chuckles, a sitcom affair,
While craters debate how to style their hair.
Moonbeams trade jokes, in gentle delight,
As dreams ride bicycles into the night.

Echoes of Cosmic Love

In the night sky, lovebirds tweet,
Sending signals, a cosmic meet.
Stars giggle in twinkling rhyme,
Planetary love, oh so sublime.

Mars winks at Venus with flair,
While Jupiter spins with a cheeky stare.
Galaxies dance, a swirling sight,
In this universe, love feels just right.

Heartbeats Across the Universe

With each pulse, stardust flies,
Alien giggles fill the skies.
A comet's tail says, 'Hey, you!'
While black holes yawn, feeling blue.

Neptune plays a ukulele tune,
While Saturn dances in a polka moon.
Echoes of hearts in a grand ballet,
Across the cosmos, they laugh and sway.

The Language of Celestial Bodies

Asteroids whisper, moons roll their eyes,
While witty meteors fall from the skies.
Stars flirt in constellations arranged,
Telling tales of love, slightly deranged.

A supernova bursts, a bright punchline,
While comets chase each other in line.
The Milky Way giggles, oh what a show,
In this cosmic chat, love starts to glow.

Astral Affection

Galactic hugs in a spiral embrace,
Love's just a wink in this vast space.
Nebulas blush with colors so bright,
Spreading affection all through the night.

Loving the planets, each twist, each turn,
In the cosmic game, there's much to learn.
With laughter and joy, we float above,
In this wild universe, we find our love.

Love's Journey Across the Heavens

We soared on clouds of whipped cream,
On dandelion seeds, we'd gleam.
With giggles shared in meteor showers,
We danced through space for hours.

But then a comet stole our fries,
We chased it down with starry eyes.
The Milky Way was our fine diner,
Who knew love could be so much finer?

Caught in a cosmic traffic jam,
Each honk echoed our love's grand slam.
We laughed as planets spilled their drinks,
In space, no one cares what planet thinks!

Through black holes and cosmic seams,
We stitched together our wildest dreams.
With a wink and nod from Mars' great chief,
We sailed the stars in disbelief.

Celestial Artistry of the Heart

Our hearts brush-stroked in lunar light,
Painting giggles through the night.
With every twinkle, a wacky smile,
Romance spread out like a comet's mile.

The sun sang tunes while Pluto danced,
In every move, we took a chance.
A canvas stretched 'neath cosmic beams,
Creating laughter in our dreams.

We crafted wishes from starry fluff,
Yet tangled up in love was tough.
With Venus' wink and Neptune's grin,
We twirled until we fell back in.

Through hues of joy and cosmic art,
The universe played its charming part.
Our love, a masterpiece galore,
In stellar chaos, we found more.

Hymns of the Solstice Skies

As Solstice dawned with playful cheer,
We sang our heart out, loud and clear.
Jupiter chuckled with a brightened blaze,
While Saturn spun in a dizzying craze.

Our love hymn echoed through the space,
Tickling comets at a lightning pace.
The stars clapped hands in frosty air,
While we made snowmen without a care.

The sun dipped low, a golden tease,
As we tumbled through the cosmic breeze.
With every wish thrown to the night,
A giggle bloomed, a pure delight.

Astral songs of love resound,
In every twirl, new joy is found.
With space as our stage, the stars aligned,
In laughter's embrace, we were entwined.

A Cosmic Tapestry of Yearning

We wove our stories through endless space,
Threads of humor in every place.
With titanic stitches, we made it clear,
Love transcends every cosmic sphere.

But oh, those threads were quite a riot,
With mischief galore turned us into a diet.
Stars became our snack attack,
As we plopped down on a meteor track.

Reciting jokes to the moonlit sky,
Our laughter echoed, oh my, oh my!
Dancing on asteroids, pirouettes in flight,
Two cosmic clowns in the sparkling night.

With every bump in our starry route,
We laughed away each cosmic doubt.
In this grand tapestry, bold and bright,
Our hearts stitched together, pure delight.

Reflections in the Cosmic Waters

In the galaxy's shimmering glare,
A fish in space does a curious stare,
'This isn't water, it's stardust soup!'
Laughs a comet, while doing a loop.

Planets spin with a wobble and twirl,
Asteroids dance, giving moons a whirl,
"What's the catch?" they giggle in flight,
"Free snacks on Mars, what a cosmic night!"

A star hiccups, sending light beams afar,
While a space worm tries to be a star,
"I can shine!" it cries, causing such a fuss,
But it's just a glow from a nuclear bus.

Each twinkle up high has a tale to tell,
Of meteor showers that rang like a bell,
So next time you gaze at the night's display,
Remember the laughter in the Milky Way.

Caresses in the Nebula Mist

In a nebula thick with cotton candy,
Two space gnomes find the atmosphere dandy,
"Careful," warns one, "that stardust can bite!"
"Then let's tickle it back!" they chuckle with delight.

A supernova sneezes, oh what a sight!
Sending starlings soaring, a comical flight,
"Catch me if you can!" yells a shooting star,
While a pancake planet comes rolling from far.

"Whispers of love are wrapped in this glow,"
Sings a heartbeat from deep within the flow,
"Floating in fumes, this universe is bold,
But our laughter's the key, it's worth its weight in gold!"

In the misty embrace of cosmic air,
Every playful giggle adds to the flair,
So dance with your shadows, sway with the beams,
The universe cuddles us within our dreams.

Luminescent Tales from Beyond

From a distant star, a tale unwinds,
A cosmic jester plays tricks on blind minds,
"Why did the black hole break up with its date?"
"Too much drama! It couldn't handle the weight!"

Zipping through galaxies with a wink and a grin,
Aliens perform with a banjo and spin,
"Join us, dear Earthlings, for a foot-tapping show,
We've got space tacos and zero-gravity dough!"

A quasar giggles, spilling its light,
While a group of meteors skates through the night,
"Oh look, a shooting star—make a wish," they cheer,
"Just make sure it's silly, we'll bring the good cheer!"

So gather your dreams, let laughter ignite,
In the cosmic corners where giggles take flight,
With tales from beyond, let joy be your guide,
In this luminescent space of our universal ride.

Starbound Enigmas of Affection

Navigating love in a cosmic trail,
A robot fell hard for a shooting male,
"Did you just pass by, or did I combust?"
"Either way, darling, it's stellar—trust!"

A wormhole giggles as planets unite,
Gifting silly vows in the glittering night,
"Across the void, I'll bring you a star,
But I might need a lift—can you take me that far?"

Whispers of data stream down from the skies,
As asteroids roll with mischievous sighs,
"What's love?" asks a comet with an awkward spin,
"Just a flare in my tail, and we're all in!"

So twirl in the cosmos, embrace the unknown,
In starbound enigmas, let affection be shown,
With laughter and wonders that glitter and shine,
In this vast universe, our hearts intertwine.

Dreamscapes Beneath the Cosmic Veil

In the sky, a cow jumps high,
Lunar cheese for all to try.
Shooting stars take silly dives,
As giggling comets do their jives.

Aliens dance with rubber shoes,
In their world, they sing the blues.
Rocket ships go zooming past,
While silly wishes sail at last.

Planets spin in disco lights,
While asteroids have pillow fights.
Galactic friends exchange a wink,
And all the stars begin to blink.

Dreamscape dreams we can all share,
In this space where humor's rare.
Floating through the endless night,
Laughter shines, a comic sight.

Love's Eclogue in the Cosmic Sea

A fish in space wears lots of flair,
With polka dots and crazy hair.
It flirts with stars, oh, what a tease,
As moons roll by with graceful ease.

Kissing comets, oh, how sweet,
While quasars wiggle to the beat.
Galaxy friends pop popcorn bright,
With supernova treats tonight.

Floating hearts and icy dreams,
Whisper soft through cosmic beams.
Planets blush, they sway and sway,
In this dance of love's bouquet.

Laughter wrapped in starlit glee,
In the vast, expansive sea.
Cosmic love wears goofy hats,
With giggles shared like playful chats.

Celestial Whispers of Romance

Stars play games of peek-a-boo,
While moons giggle in shades of blue.
Eclipses wink at lovers near,
As space gremlins cheer with a beer.

Asteroids toss love notes around,
While planets waltz, making a sound.
Rocket love with engines bright,
Zooming through the fun-filled night.

Galaxies spin goofy tales,
Shooting stars sail funky gales.
In this vast, enchanted space,
Humor flutters with each embrace.

Whispers wrapped in cosmic light,
Make even the black holes feel bright.
Laughter echoes through the skies,
Where love and joy are never shy.

Midnight Musings Under Planetary Light

A purple moon grins wide with glee,
While Saturn's rings hum a silly spree.
Galactic critters toss confetti,
As midnight serenades grow petty.

Starlit secrets shared with cheer,
As comic stars float ever near.
In the glow of laughter bright,
Midnight giggles take their flight.

Venus blushes, shy yet bold,
With tales of love, both warm and cold.
Meteor showers splash with fun,
As cosmic jokes are softly spun.

Chasing dreams with twinkling eyes,
Beneath the laughter of the skies.
In this cosmic dance of night,
Every star smiles, shining bright.

Celestial Blossoms

In the sky, a flower danced,
A comet whirled in a prance.
Stars giggled, bouncing on beams,
Sneaking kisses like silly dreams.

Asteroids wore funky hats,
Jupiter hula-hooped with chats.
Galaxies formed a conga line,
Neptune clapped; it was divine!

Moonbeams twinkled with glee,
Creating laughter for all to see.
Planets played hide and seek,
While Saturn took a selfie chic.

In this garden of cosmic cheer,
Love sprouted without any fear.
A bouquet of joy in space so vast,
Floral antics made moments last.

Illuminated Passions

A sunbeam teased a lunar glow,
Plotting mischief that stole the show.
Venus winked with a sparkling eye,
Twirling starlight, my oh my!

Shooting stars raced for the best seat,
While constellations tapped their feet.
A meteor shower brought a smile,
As lovers discoed in cosmic style.

Galactic whispers, oh so silly,
Made comets giggle, oh what a frilly!
Planetary pranks lit up the night,
Love's a dance, I guess that's right!

In moonlit laughter, hearts take flight,
Illuminated dreams shine so bright.
Cupid's arrows twirl and sway,
In this playful cosmic ballet.

The Gravity of Affection

Oh, what a pull you've got on me,
Like a black hole's tight decree.
We orbit 'round with such delight,
Defying space and laughing bright.

Your smile's a force, it makes me spin,
As planets tumble, we both grin.
I trip on stardust, but it's just fine,
With you, my star, I'll always shine.

We rocket through this love parade,
With silly antics, never delayed.
Gravity's laws can take a seat,
While we twirl in love's rhythm, sweet!

In the cosmic dance, we find our place,
A humorous waltz through infinite space.
With every laugh, we're evermore,
Bound by love's stellar core.

Celestial Harmony

In a galaxy of giggles and glee,
Where stardust tickles, just wait and see.
Planets harmonize in cosmic choir,
With melodies that never tire.

Uranus jokes, while Mercury sings,
Saturn plays bass with all kinds of strings.
A nebula whispers secrets so sweet,
In this symphony, we find our beat.

Love orbits round in a rhythmic spin,
Winning hearts with a cheeky grin.
Solar flares add sparks to the tune,
As we waltz under a beaming moon.

Cosmic laughter wraps 'round us tight,
Creating joy in the endless night.
In harmony, we float along,
Together, always—where we belong.

Starry-Eyed Whispers of the Soul

In the sky, the stars do wink,
While I sip my cosmic drink.
Planets giggle, moons play fair,
Do you think they really care?

A comet's tail, like hair in a breeze,
Plays with gravity, it's quite the tease.
Saturn laughs, rings bling-bling,
Oh, what joy the night can bring!

Galaxies spinning, a dance of fate,
But my love life feels like a plate.
Food for thought, but where's the date?
Send me signs! It's getting late!

Starry eyes, a wish on high,
Why'd I trip over that pie?
Gravity's a foe to romance,
But the universe knows how to dance.

Romance Among the Celestial Bodies

Venus blushes, is it just me?
Or is that a cosmic mishap spree?
Mars spills soda, makes a scene,
While Jupiter laughs, like it's a routine.

Uranus winks, quite the trickster,
Pluto's icy, yet feels like a mixer.
Asteroids roll like they're out on a date,
But nobody arrives—oh, the fate!

Starlit love notes dropped from above,
Echoes of laughter, a tone of love.
Quasars hum the sweetest song,
Invisible ink where we belong.

Cosmic couples keep it light,
With shooting stars, a brilliant sight.
Each twinkle carries a spark of cheer,
As I search for my date with a beer.

A Cosmic Ballet of Hearts

Dancing planets meet in a swirl,
Asteroids twirl, such a joyful whirl.
With costumes made of dust and light,
They take the stage in the velvet night.

Neptune glides with a watery grace,
While comets chase in a wild race.
An alien couple joins the fun,
Their moves are quirky, but oh, so done!

Stars applaud with a twinkling glow,
A funny dance that steals the show.
Galactic giggles fill the air,
As gravity pulls us, unaware.

A love that sparkles, twists, and spins,
In the cosmos, where the laughter wins.
With each pirouette, a joy to share,
Cosmic ballet, if only you were there.

The Dance of Fates

In the ballroom of stars, they slip and slide,
Gravity plays the DJ, can't take a ride.
Two left feet on this cosmic floor,
Tripping over dreams, what a galactic chore.

A comet dips low, a twirl goes astray,
Rocket boots malfunction, oh what a display.
They laugh and giggle with celestial grace,
Who knew the Milky Way had such a funny face?

Jupiter kicks up, chaos in the air,
Mars throws confetti, without a single care.
As planets collide, they're throwing shade,
It's a dance of fates, with cosmic charades.

But when the music stops, they'll bow and beam,
Stars wink in tune, living the dream.
Together they shimmer, beyond time's bend,
In this zany waltz, the universe amends.

Star-Crossed Echoes

Beneath the vast night, two stars collide,
With cosmic giggles, they drift and glide.
Whispers of dreams, they play pretend,
What a comedy, on this they depend.

A joke sent from Mars, in light years it flies,
Echoing laughter across endless skies.
But Venus waxed grand, with a wink and a jest,
She took the punchline and wore it the best.

Saturn's rings shake, dropping celestial bling,
As comets race past, trying to sing.
With each silly pun, they find their way,
Star-crossed echoes brighten the night's ballet.

In the tapestry of galaxies, they tease and jest,
For laughter's the guidance that makes them feel blessed.
As they frolic and tumble, amidst the stardust trails,
No tragedy here, it's laughter that prevails.

Radiance of the Heart

In the glow of twilight, hearts start to prance,
Celestial bodies join in a merry dance.
With hearts made of starlight, they twinkle and spin,
A playful affair where laughter begins.

Nebulae bloom with glittering glee,
Radiating joy, as bright as can be.
But hold on a second, what's that they see?
A planet in PJs, just sipping some tea.

Comets racing by, leaving trails of delight,
While asteroids giggle, not worried of flight.
Each heartbeat a rhythm, a cosmic thrum,
In this radiant ballet, they all become fun.

With every beat shared, they light up the night,
A constellation of chuckles, shining so bright.
In the warmth of the cosmos, they find their reward,
The radiance of hearts is the best kind of chord.

Enchanted Constellations

In a tapestry woven with fibers of dreams,
The constellations chatter with twinkling beams.
Orion forgot where he laid down his bow,
Stumbling through stardust, putting on quite a show.

Cassiopeia's crown, a bit askew,
She laughs at her reflection in the Milky Way's blue.
While Leo the lion has lost his mane,
Chasing after comets in a light-hearted game.

Shooting stars race, with giggles and cheers,
In their silky trails, they erase all fears.
With every flash of light, a joke's gently made,
In these enchanted skies, fun never will fade.

So gather round stargazers, don't let them depart,
Join in on the magic, let laughter impart.
For in every shimmer, there's a story to tell,
Enchanted constellations do all laugh so well.

Secrets of the Milky Way

Stars play hide and seek at night,
While comets zoom with all their might.
Aliens dine on cheese and bread,
Telling tales of space—what a spread!

Planets swirl in a waltz so grand,
Jupiter tries to dance but can't stand.
Saturn's rings get stuck in a knot,
While Mars snickers, "Oh, what a plot!"

Black holes munch on time and space,
While meteors run a shiny race.
Galaxies giggle, oh what a view,
Cosmic pranks, just for a few.

In this dome of starlit cheer,
Moonwalkers dance with no fear.
Life's but a cosmic jest on display,
In the laughter of the Milky Way.

Lullabies of the Cosmos

The sun hums softly, a lullaby sweet,
While planets spin, they tap their feet.
Stars in pajamas count sheep made of light,
Orbiting dreams till the morning is bright.

Asteroids sing with a clunky old tune,
Bouncing around like a joyful cartoon.
Satellites whisper secrets they've found,
As galaxies sway, all round and round.

In the quiet night of the cosmic sea,
Nebulas swirl, oh so carefree.
"Close your eyes!" chirps a comet, with glee,
As sleepy stardust drifts, wild and free.

So snuggle tight beneath cosmic covers,
Dream of space, and all its wonders.
With laughter echoing through every day,
Sleep tight, dear star, in the Milky Way.

Dreaming in Nebulae

In the soft mist of colorful puffs,
Twirly whirly space beings play rough.
They bounce on clouds of shimmering hues,
Trading their giggles for cosmic views.

A porcupine star tries to dance,
But keeps poking holes in the space-time pants.
Galactic balloons float high and bold,
Popping with laughter—a sight to behold.

Whispers of wonder in starlit streams,
Wrap around antics and nebulous dreams.
Here, every asteroid plays hide and seek,
While meteors write in scribbles so geek.

In dreaming realms where joy takes flight,
Cosmic giggles fill up the night.
So let's twirl through stars, loud and clear,
Till the dawn brings a fresh atmosphere.

Petals on Planetary Paths

Whimsical petals dance on the breeze,
Strolling on planets that wiggle with ease.
Venus has flowers that giggle and bloom,
Spreading sunshine and joy in every room.

Mars wears a cap made of twinkling lights,
Holding a party on interstellar nights.
Neptune sings softly, a lullaby sweet,
As flowers join in, tapping their feet.

Jupiter's garden, a sight full of glee,
Where veggies play games, oh look, there's a bee!
Pluto waves shyly from far away,
Planning a gathering for another day.

With petals of laughter in all grown-up styles,
Let's skip through the cosmos and share beaming smiles.
A fun fair of flowers, where joy never lacks,
Petals on paths, and no time for cracks.

Rhythms of the Interstellar Dance

Aliens groove to a funky beat,
Twisting their arms, tapping their feet.
With Martian moves and Venus winks,
They dance till they spill their cosmic drinks.

Stars are shining like disco balls,
Galactic parties have no walls.
While comets fly by in bright flashes,
The universe laughs as it crashes!

Uranus spins in a cheeky way,
While Saturn sports rings in a grand display.
Neptune chuckles, "You call that a do?"
"Try my curls, I swear they'll woo!"

So join the fun, let the planets sway,
In this zany dance where we laugh and play.

Celestial Secrets in the Ether

Mars told a joke that made stars burst,
While Mercury melted, with laughter immersed.
Jupiter sighed, "That tickles my moons,"
Glorious gas giants sharing their tunes.

Venus replied, with a wink so sly,
"I've got secrets that could make you cry!"
The stars all giggled, twinkling so bright,
As the cosmos began their roast of the night.

A black hole yawned, "I'm the main event!"
As galaxies spun with laughter, unbent.
Asteroids jived like wild confetti,
While planets took turns to be petty.

Cosmic whispers flowed like a breeze,
Who knew space could be filled with such tease?

Melodies of Cosmic Longing

In the silence of space, a tune goes by,
A quasar croons under a starry sky.
Planets grumbled, "Where's our playlist's range?"
As meteors fell, making their change.

Neptune sang low with a sultry voice,
While Saturn's rings would twirl and rejoice.
They harmonized with a great big swish,
Making the night sky their music dish.

Asteroids kept beat with a bop and a roll,
While comets joined in with a fiery stroll.
"Don't forget the chorus," cried out a star,
"We need more giggles from near and far!"

Even black holes spun to the catchy sound,
With a cosmic vibe that's truly profound.

Starlight Serenade of Desire

Shooting stars wink with romantic flair,
While lovebirds serenade in the cosmic air.
In a nebula, romance blooms so bright,
With firefly dreams that take flight at night.

The Milky Way twirls in a satin dress,
While space dust whispers, "We're truly blessed!"
Venus and Mars began a sweet fight,
Over who can croon the best moonlight.

Galactic love notes float through the void,
While stardust lovers are endlessly deployed.
Each kiss sends ripples through great infinity,
In this cosmic play, there's no need for divinity.

So dance with the stars, let your heart soar,
In the universe's arms, forever explore.

Love's Dance Amidst the Cosmic Winds

In the cosmos, hearts collide,
Like comets on a whimsical ride.
Stars giggle as they twirl about,
While planets play a love-themed bout.

Jupiter winks, and Saturn sighs,
Mars wears a robe made of cosmic pies.
Venus throws a glittering glance,
While Earth joins in the silly dance.

Galaxies spin in a giddy spree,
Charging cosmic fees for a lattice of glee.
Nebulae chuckle, bright and bold,
As they weave tales of lovers untold.

In this cosmic swirl so bright,
Laughter echoes through the night.
With each twinkle, love's jests expand,
In the vastness where dreams are planned.

Astral Fables of Desire

Amongst the stars, lovers meet,
With flirty comments, oh so sweet.
The Milky Way serves ice cream treats,
While supernovae stomp their feet.

Cosmic cats sing lullabies,
As asteroids wink with sparkly eyes.
Black holes draw in love's delight,
Swirling hearts with all their might.

Neptune fancies a dancing queen,
While comets chase with a silly sheen.
Constellations weave tales that cheer,
Shooting stars giggle, bringing near.

In this galaxy, laughter lifts,
As love's a game of playful gifts.
So grab a star and hold on tight,
In this astral tale of pure delight!

Harmonics of the Heavenly Choir

The moon strums chords on her bright lute,
As stardust dances in a cute suit.
Planets clap in rhythmic tune,
While comets hum a secret rune.

Orbits twist in gleeful sounds,
Where love's melody knows no bounds.
Jovial echoes float through the night,
As angels giggle in pure delight.

Shooting stars become the band,
Tunes of magnetism so grand.
With laughter glowing through the sky,
Love's silly song is never shy.

Harmony builds with each sweet note,
As galaxies join and sing and float.
In the cosmic choir, we find our place,
In melodies that time won't erase.

Celestial Euphoria in Quiet Moments

In quiet spaces, love's whispers bloom,
Over silent moons where stardust loom.
Galaxies chuckle, oh so divine,
As hearts pulse in a cosmic line.

Whirling planets sway with glee,
Tickling stars as they spin and flee.
In the stillness, laughter flows,
In cosmic corners, everybody knows.

And while the universe turns with grace,
Silly hearts find a brightened space.
With whispered giggles, love's a game,
In the celestial dance, we claim our fame.

So let the night wear its funny mask,
In a cosmic jest, we flirt and bask.
In these moments, euphoria reigns,
As love spins sweetly in the cosmic chains.

Love's Astral Journey.

A comet zooms through skies so bright,
I waved at it, and lost my sight.
It winked at me and said with glee,
"I hope you land on Mars, not me!"

The stars are dating, oh what a sight,
Constellations twirled, what a cosmic fright.
They danced and pranced in stellar glow,
While I tripped on a space rock below.

A meteor shower rained down like confetti,
I caught one—it felt a bit sweaty.
"Let's make wishes!" I declared with cheer,
But forgot, my purse is still in the rear!

In this galaxy, Cupid's a bug,
With arrows that often need a shrug.
For love in space can be quite absurd,
Like sending a text that never was heard.

Echoes of the Celestial Muse

The moon's got jokes, oh what a hoot,
It whispered softly, "Try a new suit!"
I laughed so hard, I floated away,
Bouncing on stardust, hip-hip-hooray!

Saturn's rings are quite the affair,
They threw a party, we danced in the air.
But my dance moves got me all dizzy,
I collided with Pluto—oh so frizzy!

The sun is a diva, always in rays,
It demands attention in so many ways.
I waved to it, but got burned instead,
Next time I'll stick to just saying "hey!" instead.

A black hole pulled me into its charm,
I thought I'd enjoy, but it was a harm.
"You're too intense!" I started to pout,
And in a whirl, I got spat back out!

Serenade of the Starlit Heart

Starlight glimmers, a romantic dance,
I tried to impress, but lost my pants.
As meteors fell like confetti delights,
I realized quick, love's not all heights!

An alien smiled, offered me a drink,
But it was goo—what's this, I stink?
We laughed it off, what a cosmic blend,
A friendship forged, out of goo we'd send.

The planets gossip behind our backs,
"What's he got? A galactic knack?"
I just shrugged, with a cosmic grin,
Sometimes love is just about the spin!

Cosmic serenades, oh how they hum,
Even black holes can't quiet the fun.
In love's great scheme, we find our way,
With laughter brightening up the day!

Whispers in the Cosmic Garden

In a garden of stars, I planted a joke,
A flower bloomed with a saturated poke.
It giggled and shimmered in the twilight glow,
"You're the funniest traveler I ever did know!"

Galactic critters all gathered near,
With tiny ears, they fluffed up with cheer.
They whispered secrets of love and delight,
While flying saucers zipped left and right.

Asteroids chirped, they danced on the lane,
Though one tried to tango and spun in vain.
"Watch your footwork!" I hollered aloud,
"Love's not a dance if you're tripping the crowd!"

In this cosmic garden of twinkling lights,
Harmony blossomed on laughter-filled nights.
So here's to the beacons, the comets that gleam,
In the universe's chaos, we live our dream!

Celestial Echoes

Up in the sky, a wink from the Moon,
The planets dance like they're in a tune.
Jupiter slurps from a cosmic cup,
While Saturn laughs, saying, "Hey, let's sup!"

Mars trips over its own little dust,
Makes the whole Milky Way giggle, we must.
Comets are jester with tails all aflame,
In this cosmic circus, it's all just a game!

A nebula's sigh sounds like a big joke,
While Mercury winks as it spins like a bloke.
Galaxies spin, what a silly ballet,
Where stars nudge each other and giggle all day!

With every new light, there's laughter so bright,
In cosmic confetti, they dance through the night.
The universe chuckles, its heart full of cheer,
Saying, "Why take life seriously? It's better here!"

Whispers of the Night Sky

In the darkness, the stars play charades,
Orion's new dance was a viral parade.
The Night Owl hoots, he's the judge of it all,
While the Milky Way giggles, ready to sprawl.

Venus winks slyly, a cheeky old tease,
Singing sweet nothings to a passing breeze.
The Moon whispers secrets, a playful affair,
As comets sweep by, their laughter in air!

Every twinkle's a chuckle, a cosmic reply,
Echoes of giggles float high in the sky.
Asteroids tumble, all clumsy and rude,
Spreading their joy like a space-faring food!

A star sneezes glitter, a tickle of light,
While space pets frolic—from day until night.
So up in the heavens, where laughter is king,
Join in the fun, let your joy freely sing!

Starlit Serenades

The stars start to croon, oh what a delight,
Singing for space cows in their cosmic night flight.
Neptune's on harmonica, plucking along,
While Pluto claps paws to our giggly song.

In orbit, they waltz with a shimmy and shake,
A galaxy of laughter, for goodness' sake!
Saturn spins much faster, its rings made of cheese,
Chasing down the meteors, hoping to please.

Shooting stars whisper their funniest tales,
Hitchhiking comets leave behind cosmic trails.
Jupiter's laughing, with moons like a crew,
Playing hopscotch with stardust, keep it in view!

The universe dances, a jig filled with glee,
Winking at us; it's a spectacle, see?
So join in the fun, let your spirit take flight,
In the starlit serenades of the night!

Ode to the Morning Star

Oh, Morning Star, you rise with a grin,
Winking at night like you're just coming in.
You shake off the dreams with a twinkle of sass,
While sleepy-eyed planets begin to amass.

"Good morning!" you shout, with a radiant glow,
While the Sun, still yawning, starts stealing the show.
Venus giggles softly, still wrapped in her sheets,
Hiding her smile as the new day repeats.

Your beams chase away all the fuzzy night fears,
And tickle the clouds while igniting cheers.
The cosmos erupts in a jubilant play,
As twilight gives way to the dawning array!

There's laughter in beams, as they shimmer and sway,
Your joy paints the sky in a whimsical way.
So here's to the giggles, the fun of your start,
Oh, radiant being, we cherish your heart!

Fables in the Twilight of the Universe

In the glow of an alien moon,
A cat danced with a spoon.
Stars giggled at the sight,
As noodles soared into the night.

Planets played hide and seek,
While comets gave a cheeky peek.
Galaxies twirled in a drunken spin,
While Martians tossed their gin.

Saturn's rings caught a fishy tale,
As a wolf howled without fail.
Laughter echoed through the skies,
Even asteroids wore surprise eyes.

So here's a toast from space so wide,
To all the twinkling stars that glide.
May our fables soar and spin,
Where the universe lets the fun begin.

Poetic Orbits of the Heart

In a galaxy where dreams collide,
Cupid lost his arrow and cried.
Planets whirled in a playful dance,
While asteroids flirted in a cosmic chance.

Venus wore a sassy grin,
Dressed in stardust, ready to win.
With winks and nods, she aimed so true,
But shot a fish instead, who knew?

Distant moons teased each other's glow,
Throwing glitter like a wild show.
Stars whispered secrets, oh so dear,
As the universe giggled, never fear.

So if your heart feels a little strange,
Just look to the skies, it's all deranged.
In this poetic orbit, love's a game,
Where laughter and joy are always the same.

Revelations Under the Stellar Canopy

Beneath the stars, we shared a snack,
With aliens plotting a little jab.
Galactic whispers floated around,
As flying pigs danced on the ground.

UFOs joined in on the fun,
With laser lights, they made a pun.
The Milky Way played hide and seek,
While silly jokes made planets tweak.

Cosmic cats stretched with delight,
As meteorites fell in the night.
Secrets exchanged in waves of light,
With laughter ringing, oh so bright.

So let us savor this stellar feast,
Where humor and wonder never cease.
In this cosmic giggle, we find our way,
Under the canopy, where we can play.

Echoes of an Astral Embrace

In the vastness, a comet did sneeze,
Sending laughter through soft, starry breeze.
Galaxies hugged with a warm delight,
Spreading chuckles all through the night.

Neptune wore pants that were quite bizarre,
While Jupiter couldn't find his car.
Ringing auroras made faces galore,
As cosmic beings chattered and swore.

With a wink and a jiggle, the cosmos spun,
Creating mischief until we were done.
Through echoes of laughter, we play and explore,
In the great astral embrace that we adore.

So if you're feeling a bit out of place,
Just join the dance in this limitless space.
Where humor reigns and joy takes the lead,
In echoes of stars, there's all that we need.

Sonnet of the Celestial Rose

A rose so bright in outer space,
Floats around with a silly grace.
It tickles stars, and giggles too,
Winking down at me and you.

In cosmic gardens, laughter blooms,
As comets sweep through cheerful rooms.
With every twirl, the planets dance,
A cosmic ball, with twinkling pants!

Aliens join in playful jest,
At starlit picnics, they're the best.
With frosty snacks and noodle soup,
They all sit down for one big loop.

So when you dream of love so grand,
Just peek above at the starry band.
For joy is hid in lunar light,
Where even asteroids delight.

Love Notes Beneath the Milky Way

Underneath a sky so bright,
I scribble notes in sheer delight.
They float like petals on the breeze,
To find you lost among the trees.

Each star a wink, a smile, a sigh,
I toss my paper plane up high.
It sails through cosmic winds with glee,
But lands, alas, in a honey tree!

Bees buzz 'round, with letters stuck,
While I just laugh, what silly luck!
They share my tales with lots of sting,
Transforming love to a buzzing fling.

Yet still I smile as skies swirl bright,
For even bees may find delight.
Through every laugh and poet's play,
We find our love beneath the sway.

Lullabies of the Eternal Night

In the depths where stardust dreams,
Sleepy planets giggle and gleam.
They whisper jokes, like hidden spells,
As space cows moo across star wells.

Moonbeams rock the sleepy sun,
While planets play leapfrog and run.
Nebulae swirl with tickling sighs,
Daring black holes to spin and rise.

Galaxies giggle, like playful sprites,
They toss around some twinkling lights.
In this lull of cosmic game,
The universe is never the same.

So close your eyes, and out of sight,
Find joy in this eternal night.
For as you dream of endless flight,
The cosmos laughs, and it feels right.

Starlit Confessions

A comet dashes, bold and bright,
With secrets shared in soft moonlight.
'I've loved this star,' it squeals with glee,
While suns turn sassy, full of spree.

A satellite, with flair and class,
Shares tales of planets eating grass.
'It's quite a sight,' it laughs and sighs,
'When Jupiter wears those silly ties!'

The rings of Saturn twirl and spin,
They host a dance where none can win.
With laughter echoing through the void,
Each twinkle, tease, and light deployed.

So gather 'round, all stars and moons,
Dive deep into the cosmic tunes.
For in this dark, where joy confesses,
The universe lives with such excesses.

Chasing Comets of the Soul

I chased a comet through the night,
My hair went wild, what a sight!
It winked at me, then took a turn,
I tumbled down, oh how I yearn!

With space snacks packed, I soared so high,
A pizza planet caught my eye.
I took a slice, it flew away,
My cosmic diet gone astray!

Chasing those trails of starry cheer,
I found a dance floor up in here.
The moons all laughed, they set the beat,
My feet got tangled, what a feat!

So here I am, with stardust jam,
A comet struck, I lost my pram.
But in this chase, I find my glee,
An endless ride through fantasy!

Sublime Harmonies of the Cosmos

In cosmic tunes, I found a note,
A melody that made me float.
The planets sang of cheese and pie,
I laughed so hard, I touched the sky!

With every strum on starry strings,
The universe shared its wild flings.
A lunar love song played so sweet,
I danced in circles on my feet!

They say the stars have rhythm too,
But all they do is play peekaboo.
I joined their song, we laughed together,
A galactic choir, light as feather!

So take a chance, join the swell,
In space's orchestra, all is well.
With jingles bright, we make a scene,
A silly trip through skies so keen!

Astral Visions of Unseen Passions

I saw a star, it winked so sly,
It tossed a note, said 'come and fly!'
With cosmic dreams of love abloom,
I tripped and stumbled, hit the moon!

In swirling gas, I found a friend,
A quirky quasar with no end.
We spun like whirlwinds, lost in play,
Arguing which way was the Milky Way!

A shooting star sent out a call,
It dared me to take a cosmic fall.
I took a leap, and oh, what fun!
Fell into laughter, my heart undone!

So here we drift, through space and time,
Chasing visions, all in rhyme.
Unseen passions paint the dark,
A silly spark igniting the arc!

Sculpting Dreams in the Cosmic Canvas

With starlight paint, I made a mess,
A galactic picture, I confess.
The comets laughed, they joined the art,
As I splattered dreams with all my heart!

I sculpted moons from distant clay,
Each shaped with giggles on display.
A playful star took on a grin,
And danced around as I pulled it in!

The nebula joined in the fun,
Twisting colors, a rainbow run.
My canvas bloomed with laughter loud,
It's cosmic chaos, bold and proud!

So grab your brush and take a chance,
In this universe, let's do a dance.
With dreams to sculpt and stars to spin,
The art of laughter will always win!

Chants of the Ethereal Realm

In the land where stars wear hats,
And dancing comets chase the bats.
The moon hops like a bouncy ball,
While planets giggle, having a ball.

Rockets slip on cosmic ice,
Trying to impress, oh how nice!
But they wobble and they spin,
Creating laughter, where to begin?

Harmonies from the Planetary Veil

Saturn rings with a silly tune,
While Jupiter hums under the moon.
A meteor tonight has lost its way,
Laughing as it turns into ballet.

Venus wears a polka-dotted dress,
And Mars plays the spoons, oh what a mess!
Comets try a wiggly dance,
Leave the universe in a trance.

Celestial Ballads and Lunar Dreams

A star sneezes and twirls around,
While nebulae giggle without a sound.
A space cat chases a laser beam,
In the cosmos, nothing's as it seems.

The sun jokes with the earth so bright,
Whispers secrets that tickle the night.
Planets tell tales of their grand spree,
Spinning in circles, as happy as can be.

Echoing Hearts Beyond the Horizon

In the pocket of the Milky Way,
Stars play cards and hold their sway.
Constellations crack jokes in the dark,
While black holes snicker, leaving a mark.

With meteors racing in a rare feat,
They high-five each other, oh what a treat!
The universe spins in a silly whirl,
With giggles and tickles, let laughter unfurl.

Ethereal Echoes in Silver Skies

In the night, a comet zooms,
Chasing cupcakes on silver brooms,
Stars giggle, they wink and sway,
As planets dance the Milky Way.

A love note falls from Mars to Moon,
Promising to meet up at noon,
Aliens munch on cosmic fries,
While funny little moons wear ties.

Jupiter's clowns juggle space cheese,
Shooting stars float like cotton peas,
Neptune sings a silly tune,
As the sun wears shades in a balloon.

Galaxies spin with a raucous cheer,
While asteroids share a pint of beer,
Ethereal echoes laugh and play,
In the cosmic drama of the day.

Cosmic Reverberations of Love

Astronauts giggle in zero-g,
In love with stars, it's plain to see,
They float in hearts, a cosmic jam,
While meteors roast a cosmic ham.

Venus flirts with a nearby star,
Sending out wishes with a guitar,
Comets wish they had sweethearts too,
As space dust glitters, wooing blue.

Black holes spin like a wild old cat,
Swallowing socks and a silly hat,
Gravitational pull of goofy dance,
In this universe, there's always a chance.

Saturn's rings host a wobbly fair,
With quirky rides and asteroids in air,
Cosmic echoes of love resound,
As laughter ripples all around.

Whimsies Amidst the Stars

Quasars bake star-shaped pies,
While stardust sprinkles on the flies,
Galactic friends play hopscotch right,
Under a moon that's glowing bright.

Planets trade their shiny hats,
While comets giggle, chasing cats,
With each twirl, a new jape unfurls,
In the whimsical dance of the swirls.

Aliens paint with cosmic glue,
Creating pictures in shades of blue,
With every brushstroke, laughter grows,
As space dust tickles our toes.

Bubbles float through the starlit night,
While laughter stretches to meteors' flight,
Whimsies twirl, an astral spree,
In a universe that's wild and free.

Heartstrings Plucked by the Universe

Saturn strums its golden strings,
While moonbeams dance and fun it brings,
Every note a twinkling laugh,
As wormholes sketch a cosmic path.

Nebulae tickle the solar flare,
With a cosmic band playing tunes in air,
Stars lined up with playful grace,
Creating rhythms in endless space.

Heartbeat echoes across the void,
As black holes hum, all fear destroyed,
With every pluck, a galaxy sways,
In the universe's rollicking ways.

Shooting stars take flight to the beat,
While dark matter taps its tiny feet,
Heartstrings plucked in this grand display,
As laughter reigns in a cosmic ballet.

Poetry from the Infinite Expanse

In the vastness of night, I found my shoe,
A sparkly star told me it belonged to you.
Gravity giggled, pulling my hair,
As I danced with shadows without a care.

Martians flew past, waving their hands,
While I was lost in the heart of the sands.
Cosmic hiccups made my heart race,
Aliens joined in, filling the space.

Black holes whisper secrets of fate,
One just stole my last slice of cake!
Lunar llamas leapt, such an odd sight,
Underneath comets, we played through the night.

So here's to the cosmos, absurd and bright,
Where logic bends and giggles take flight.
With each twinkling light, a chuckle ensues,
In this infinite expanse, I lost my shoes.

Twilight Hallucinations of the Heart

In the twilight's glow, I met a frog,
He recited sonnets to a smug old dog.
Moonbeams giggled, sharing their light,
As squirrels were tangoing, oh what a sight!

The stars played poker, and I lost my stake,
To a bright, shiny comet that claimed it as fate.
Jupiter chuckled, spilled juice on my dreams,
While Venus whispered in spontaneous screams.

Mistaking a shadow for my favorite snack,
I tried to eat it but got a heart attack.
Reality jumbled in hues, bold and tart,
As glittering jokes danced within my heart.

With every twinkle, the laughter ignites,
In twilight's arms, we embrace silly flights.
Here's to the quirks that make our souls dart,
In this wacky world of hallucinated art.

Hallowed Constellations of Hope

The stars convened for an evening bash,
A meteor shower led to a crash!
With galaxies giggling, all filled with cheer,
Even the sun wore its best disco gear.

Asteroids danced on their wobbly legs,
While aliens brewed interstellar pegs.
Shooting stars launched from the Milky Way,
Chasing dreams that loved to play.

In this hallowed space, I blended in,
With a nebula cat that wore a grin.
We sang silly tunes under Saturn's rings,
Imagining the joy that laughter brings.

As cosmic winds swirled, we spilled our hopes,
Creating a canvas with stellar scopes.
In every bright twinkle, a giggle we sow,
In these hallowed constellations of hope, we glow!

Fragile Moments in the Celestial Tides

In the ocean of stars, I splashed with glee,
Riding a wave on a whimsical spree.
Galactic jellyfish danced all around,
Tickling the air with joy profound.

Cosmic ripples rolled, a splendid sight,
As laughter echoed in the soft starlight.
I tried to capture the laughter I found,
But it slipped like sand into dreams unbound.

Shooting starts wobbled in comical grace,
Turning my frown into a bright, silly face.
While the moon chuckled, hiding its beams,
Caught in a whirl of whimsical dreams.

With fragile moments adrift on galactic seas,
I danced with the comets and laughed with the breeze.
In the tides of the cosmos, I found my delight,
Where the fragile and funny together unite.

Love Letters in Orbit

In a satellite's spin, the heart takes flight,
A paper airplane sails, a comical sight.
With ink that's invisible, it scribbles a deal,
A cosmic love note, with zero appeal.

Asteroids chuckle, as they pass us by,
Cupid's lost arrows go drifting awry.
In this endless void, romance does bloom,
But gravity's pull brings the chaos of doom.

Stars giggle softly, they wink and they tease,
As I trip over stardust, my knees feel the squeeze.
Through black holes and comets, our laughter does echo,
Two lovers adrift in the whims of the metro.

With a comet's tail, I send you my care,
But letters get stuck in a solar flare!
Yet still I persist, with a wink and a grin,
For love knows no bounds, nor the mess we're in.

Moonlight Melodies

Under the moon, where shadows dance free,
I serenade crickets—just you wait and see!
They chirp in confusion, it's not quite a song,
But in this lunar swamp, we both can't go wrong.

The owls roll their eyes, my pitch is quite off,
As I try to woo you with a lyrical scoff.
But look at the stars, they're laughing along,
A giggle, a twinkle, like light in a throng.

Cosmic DJ spins tunes from afar,
But my clumsy two-step won't get me that far.
Dance beneath the glow, we'll groove with delight,
In the awkward embrace of this strange lunar night.

So let's raise a toast with moonbeams and zest,
To love without rhythm, it's truly the best!
With giggles and winks in this melodic embrace,
We'll spin through our dreams in this starry place.

Cosmic Embrace

In the galaxy's arms, we swirl and we twirl,
Spinning like planets, in a messy whirl.
Your smile is bright, like a supernova's blast,
Yet my socks are mismatched, oh what a contrast!

In zero gravity, our hugs go astray,
Floating in laughter, we drift day by day.
I trip on the cosmos, you chuckle and cheer,
For love is a dance, and I'm stepping in sheer.

With meteors crashing, our dreams take a ride,
Your heart is my anchor, I can't run and hide.
But if we get lost in this vast starry stream,
At least we can giggle, it's all just a dream.

So here's to the chaos, the starlit embrace,
With quirks and with quirks, we'll find our own place.
In this wacky romance, we take off with glee,
Two comets in sync, just you wait and see!

Twilight Blossoms

In twilight's soft glow, let's frolic and play,
Petals of laughter drift gracefully away.
With pollen for kisses, the bees start to hum,
As we break out in song—what a truly bad pun!

The sun's getting lazy, it blinks down at us,
We dance in the breeze, not causing a fuss.
But watch where you step, those daisies are sly,
They tickle your toes, oh my, oh my!

The stars start to peek, through the branches they glee,
Each flower a secret, as silly as we.
So let's twirl through the garden, no cares or regrets,
For laughter's the flower that nobody pets.

Under twilight, we blossom, so wild and so free,
With giggles and whispers, just you and me.
In this garden of chaos, our spirits shall soar,
Twilight's sweet humor, who could ask for more?

Sagas of Endless Night

In the cloak of nighttime's embrace,
Stars play hide and seek in space.
Moon whispers secrets in a light jest,
While aliens laugh, trying to rest.

Galactic gasbags strut around,
In their shiny suits, they make no sound.
Space-time's a buffet, they munch with glee,
Counting black holes like count of their tea.

Shooting stars trip over their tails,
While cosmic squirrels tell silly tales.
Gravity giggles, it's dizzying fun,
Hitch a ride 'til the morning sun.

Yet comets glide with a wink and a swish,
Dreaming of planets, making a wish.
In the universe's dance, we are just a slight twist,
In this cosmic comedy, we surely exist.

Enchantments of the Starry Expanse

In the vastness of cosmic layers,
Meteors throw glitter like party players.
Planets spin tales that tickle the ear,
While stardust sneezes and brings forth cheer.

Galaxies swirl, making grand poses,
While quasars blush like red, thorny roses.
They gossip of comets with tails so long,
Chasing them all in a silly song.

Nebulae puff like clouds in a race,
Twinkling with laughter at time and space.
Asteroids bump, and oh what a scene,
Racing through stardust, all wild and keen.

In the starlit laughter, we join the jest,
With every blink, the universe is blessed.
In cosmic wonders, we dive and play,
As the stars twinkle back in their own way.

Lyrical Journeys Through the Nebula

In a nebula thick with colorful sprays,
Time wanders off in whimsical ways.
Stars get tangled in bright ribbons of fate,
While space explorers just can't wait!

They wear shiny suits and goofy grins,
Trying new dances where starlight spins.
Finding new worlds that bubble and pop,
On an intergalactic candy shop.

With aliens making odd balloon shapes,
As they point and laugh, sipping space grapes.
Every warp in time is a chance to play,
Floating on puns as they drift away.

Shooting through clouds that sparkle and beam,
Each journey unfolds like a strange dream.
In cosmic mischief, we take our flight,
Creating laughter in endless night.

Odes to the Cosmic Traveler

Oh, cosmic traveler with shoes made of stars,
Dancing through stardust, not caring how far.
Your laughter ignites like a supernova,
Bringing happiness, like a sweet coca-cola.

With a wink and a nudge from far-off Mars,
You take snapshots, while munching on bars.
Planets spin tales that bubble and burst,
Creating a ruckus in the galactic thirst.

Your laugh echoes through black holes so round,
Filling the emptiness with glittery sound.
In asteroid fields, your joy's all aflutter,
Making space sandwiches with stars and some butter.

So here's to the journeys we joyfully seek,
Paddling through comets, elusive and sleek.
With humor as fuel and wonder as guide,
In the universe's belly, we boldly glide.

Celestial Dreams Unfurled

In the cosmos, cows float by,
Mooing softly, oh my my!
Aliens giggle, on clouds they sit,
Trading jokes, never a wit.

Planets wear socks, tights, and capes,
Bouncing 'round, making shapes!
Stars wink with a playful glow,
Drawing laughter, stealing the show.

Space dogs howl to the tune of night,
Chasing comets, what a sight!
Galactic parties, zero-gravity fun,
Eclipsing boredom, one by one.

Floating toasts with meteor wine,
Sipping stardust, feeling fine!
Napping on rings, they dream and dance,
In the universe's grand romance.

Hymns of the Galactic Breeze

Jupiter sings in a comet's tail,
Pigs with wings on a moonlit trail!
Saturn spins with a starry grin,
Wearing bling from the cosmic bin.

Shooting stars make a wish or two,
While aliens prance in cosmic blue.
A nebula tickles the Milky Way,
Whispering secrets of a cosmic ballet.

Lunar bunnies hop with flair,
Pulling pranks without a care.
Galaxies giggle when twinkling bright,
Sharing the joy of a silly night.

Meteor showers bring laughter loud,
Sprinkling joy on a twinkling crowd.
With every joke, the cosmos sways,
In a symphony of silly plays.

Chasing Stardust

Chasing stardust with a wink,
Fairies giggle, sip and drink.
Glistening stars in the sky so high,
Twinkling tales as they pass by.

Asteroids wobble on laughter's breeze,
Gathers for jokes, oh what a tease!
Crafting dreams on a light beam's ride,
With cosmic giggles, all abide.

Laughter rockets through space so wide,
With floppy hats in a whimsical tide.
Chasing dawn with a fluffy cloud,
Creating moments that feel so proud.

They tumble and roll, what a sight,
With stardust wishes, all feel light.
Every twinkle a chuckle, pure delight,
In this celestial dance, oh so bright!

A Symphony of Light

A band of stars plays a joyful tune,
While planets jiggle like a cartoon.
Galactic saxophones honk and blare,
Filling the cosmos with wild flair.

Nebulous notes float on silver streams,
In the realm of cosmic dreams.
Alien choirs sing all the way,
Rocking the universe night and day.

Silly soundwaves twist and spin,
With laughter echoing from within.
Cosmic doves dance in a dazzling swoon,
Painting the night with a radiant boon.

As the sun yawns, the stars take flight,
In this orchestra of endless light.
Every giggle, a starlit thrill,
In a symphony that time can't still.

Radiant Dreams in Celestial Cascades

Amidst the stars a giggle glows,
Where cosmic beans sprout silly toes.
Strangely shaped, they dance and sway,
Chasing moons in a playful ballet.

With comets racing, laughs abound,
A cheeky sun plays peek-a-boo round.
Galactic clouds sporting silly hats,
Who knew the cosmos had such spats?

Starfish juggling on golden beams,
While Saturn pranks with endless dreams.
Whimsical whirlwinds spin and twirl,
Just cosmic mischief in a celestial swirl.

In these radiant dreams, we find delight,
Under a sky that sparkles bright.
Laughter echoes through the night,
In the universe's playful flight.

Celestial Sleigh Ride to Eternity

On stardust sleds we glide with glee,
Riding comets, wild and free.
A giggling moon leads the way,
Through velvet skies where fairies play.

Jupiter's jumpers bounce around,
Playful pranks from planets abound.
Galaxies twirl in a dance so spry,
As we slide down the Milky Way high.

With a sprinkle of joy, a dash of joy,
Even black holes can't suck our ploy.
Bumping into stars, we laugh and cheer,
As Captain Quasar steers us near.

A sleigh ride through the cosmic light,
Chasing dreams into the night.
In this eternal fun parade,
Nothing's too silly, our fears allayed.

Parables from the Starry Abyss

In the depths of the night, odd tales unfold,
Stars spin yarns of mischief bold.
A nebula sneezes, and guess what flies?
Galactic hiccups and comet pies!

Asteroids gather to share their quirks,
With whimsical winks and playful smirks.
Constellations chuckle at their own shapes,
Scattering laughter like little grapes.

Martian mimes play their tricks,
Stealing dance moves, oh, what a mix!
Each twinkle a wink, a jolly muse,
In this cosmic theater, we can't refuse.

From the starry abyss, joy resonates,
With every heartbeat, wonder relates.
In cosmic whispers, humor reigns,
Painting the universe with vibrant chains.

Celestial Ballads of Lost Love

In the cosmos, where heartstrings sing,
A love that's lost can still take wing.
Planets sigh with a gentle breeze,
While meteors weep in the cosmic freeze.

Venus twirls in a dance of glee,
Wishing on stars, oh let it be!
A comical tale of a star-crossed plight,
Lost socks spinning in the endless night.

Jupiter's heart is a whopping size,
But can't find love 'mongst swirling skies.
He flirts with each ring, but alas, he sighs,
Seeing Saturn's smile, amidst the skies.

Yet laughter lingers through every tear,
In this comedy of hearts, so dear.
Celestial ballads make grief feel light,
In the dance of stars, love shines bright.

Enigmas of Intergalactic Love

A Martian asked a Venus clone,
"What's it like to love alone?"
She giggled, rolling eyes of green,
"Throughout the stars, I'm quite the queen!"

An asteroid once tried to flirt,
But in the end, it just got hurt.
With cosmic dust, it lost all grace,
And now it drifts without a trace.

The moonbeams tried to set a date,
But every time, they were too late.
"Oh Lunar Light, you silly rock!"
"You're always stuck in yonder clock!"

Yet through the galaxy's embrace,
They laugh and twirl in endless space.
Matching photons dance and spin,
In cosmic love they always win!

The Lure of Celestial Brightness

A supernova dressed in flair,
Said, "Come closer, I'm quite rare!"
The stars all gasped, wore shades of gold,
"But bright is not the new and bold!"

A comets' tail swept through the air,
Claimed, "I've got style beyond compare!"
But black holes laughed, quite out of line,
"Your fashion's just a slushy brine!"

In telescopes the aliens peek,
To catch a wink or cheeky cheek.
A wink from Mars made Venus sneer,
"I swear those eyes are just a sphere!"

Yet all the cosmos hums a tune,
Of love that glimmers under moon.
For laughter is the brightest star,
In every heart, near and afar!

Elysian Fields in Astro-Affection

In fields of stardust, hearts collide,
Where aliens skip and fruits abide.
A shape-shifter winked, then danced around,
"With cosmic lassos, love is found!"

Mars teased Jupiter with its flair,
"Your big red storms can't match my hair!"
Jupiter just chuckled, oh so wise,
"Can you withstand my giant size?"

With laughter echoing through the void,
Two comets met, love was deployed.
They twirled and spun in a wild race,
While planets joined the joyful chase!

So spread your arms, embrace the fun,
In starlit fields where life's begun.
For in the cosmic garden's glow,
Love blossoms bright, make sure you sow!

Cosmic Threads of Affection Woven

Across the cosmos, threads entwine,
Where giggling stars and moons align.
A spaghetti-like pulsar swayed,
"I'm pasta-perfect, be not afraid!"

A nebula laughed, a swirling delight,
"Your noodle moves just aren't quite right!"
Yet every twist and every turn,
In galactic kitchens, love did burn!

A solar flare proposed a game,
"Who'll catch Cupid's dart, what a name!"
But Martians tripped, red dust a-fly,
"Is love a sport? We all wonder why!"

Yet in this dance, all beings play,
Finding humor in each way.
For in the fabric of this sphere,
A laugh is worth a million years!

www.ingramcontent.com/pod-product-compliance
Lightning Source LLC
Chambersburg PA
CBHW051647160426
43209CB00004B/823